A Timeline of Long-Distance Communication

Smoke Signals to Smartphones

WORLD BOOK

World Book
a Scott Fetzer company
Chicago

World Book, Inc.
180 North LaSalle Street
Suite 900
Chicago, Illinois 60601
USA

For information about other World Book publications, call 1-800-WORLDBK (967-5325).

For information about sales to schools and libraries, call 1-800-975-3250 (United States) or 1-800-837-5365 (Canada).

Produced for World Book, Inc. by Bailey Publishing Associates Ltd.

Library of Congress Cataloging-in-Publication Data

Title: Smoke signals to smartphones: a timeline of long-distance communication.
Description: Chicago: World Book, Inc., a Scott Fetzer company, 2016. | Series: A timeline of ... | Includes index.
Identifiers: LCCN 2016012914 | ISBN 9780716635437
Subjects: LCSH: Communication--History--Juvenile literature. | Technology--History--Juvenile literature.
Classification: LCC P96.T42 S54 2016 | DDC 302.209--dc23
LC record available at https://lccn.loc.gov/2016012914

Smoke Signals to Smartphones: A Timeline of Long-Distance Communication ISBN: 978-0-7166-3543-7
A Timeline of... Set ISBN: 978-0-7166-3539-0
E-book ISBN: 978-0-7166-3552-9 (ePUB3 format)

Printed in China by Shenzhen Wing King Tong Paper Products Co., Ltd., Guangdong Province
1st printing July 2016

Acknowledgments

Cover photo: Shutterstock (Alexander_P).

Bridgeman 6 (Archives Charmet), 8 (Look & Learn), 11 right (Belvoir Castle), 12 (Biblioteca Nazionale), 19 (Peter Newark Collection), 29.

Corbis 15 (L. de Selva), 16 right (Tarker), 17 (Dorling Kindersley), 21, 22 left, 22 right (S. Bianchetti), 25, 26 (Hulton-Deutsch Collection), 27 (Bettmann), 30 (T. Soqui), 31 (C. O'Rear), 32 left (E. Quinn), 35 (JGI/J. Grill/Blend Images).

Elisa Triolo 10.

Getty 4 top (MPI), 11 left (Florilegius/SSPL), 13 (M. Hanson), 18 left (Stock Montage), 18 right (Authenticated News), 20 (Rischgitz), 23 (Time Life), 24 left (Science & Society), 24 right (American Stock Archive), 28 (Hulton Archive), 32 right (U. Baumgarten), 33 (ullstein bild), 34 (N. Kamm/AFP), 36 left (P. Macdiarmid), 36 right (J. MacDougall/AFP).

Shutterstock 4 bottom (junpinzon), 9 (stocksolutions), 37 (L. Konuk).

Walker Art Gallery 14.

World Book 7.

Yale Center for British Art 16 left.

Staff

Writer: Alex Woolf

Executive Committee

President
Jim O'Rourke

Vice President and Editor in Chief
Paul A. Kobasa

Vice President, Finance
Donald D. Keller

Vice President, Marketing
Jean Lin

Vice President, International
Kristin Norell

Director, Human Resources
Bev Ecker

Editorial

Manager, Annuals/Series Nonfiction
Christine Sullivan

Editor, Annuals/Series Nonfiction
Kendra Muntz

Manager, Sciences
Jeff De La Rosa

Editor, Sciences
Daniel Kenis

Administrative Assistant
Annuals/Series Nonfiction
Ethel Matthews

Manager, Contracts & Compliance
(Rights & Permissions)
Loranne K. Shields

Manager, Indexing Services
David Pofelski

Digital

Director, Digital Product Content Development
Emily Kline

Director, Digital Product Development
Erika Meller

Digital Product Manager
Lyndsie Manusos

Digital Product Coordinator
Matthew Werner

Manufacturing/Production

Manufacturing Manager
Sandra Johnson

Production/Technology Manager
Anne Fritzinger

Proofreader
Nathalie Strassheim

Graphics and Design

Senior Art Director
Tom Evans

Senior Designer
Matt Carrington

Media Editor
Rosalia Bledsoe

Manager, Cartographic Services
Wayne K. Pichler

Senior Cartographer
John M. Rejba

Special thanks to:

Roberta Bailey
Nicola Barber
Ian Winton
Alex Woolf

Glossary There is a glossary of terms on page 38. Terms defined in the glossary are in type that **looks like this** (called *boldface type*) on their first appearance on any *spread* (two facing pages).

Circa Some dates are written with *c.* before the year. The *c.* stands for *circa*. Circa means *approximately.* For example, with c. 250 B.C., the phrase is read as "circa 250 B.C.," meaning *approximately 250 B.C.* Circa can be used with both B.C. and A.D. dates.

Contents

Smoke Signals to Smartphones

A Timeline of Long-Distance Communication

Ancient peoples used smoke signals to send simple messages by sight.

Today, many people enjoy instantaneous communication using smartphones, computers, and the Internet.

Introduction
Communication Through the Ages

Throughout history, people have needed to communicate over long distances. Communication is the sharing of information. In early times, people might have communicated to one another over short distances about an attacking enemy. Or they may have sent a signal about a new food source. Over time, people needed to develop methods to send messages farther and faster across the land. Today, people use long-range communication, called *telecommunications*, for work and to talk to family or friends.

The first forms of long-distance communication used signals that could be seen. Such visual signals included flags or smoke. Early people also used sound signals, such as drums or horns. Longer, more complex messages could be written down. Then a **courier** could carry and deliver the message. Couriers worked for the first postal services. Ancient empires created postal services to connect their vast lands together.

The biggest revolution in long-distance communication began in the 1800's. During this time, people learned how to send information as electrical signals. Such signals could travel through electrical wires. Or they could travel as invisible waves through the air. Electrical signals gave rise to the electric **telegraph,** telephone, radio, television, satellite communications, computers, cell phones, and the Internet. Today, we can use signals that move through the air to communicate almost instantly with anyone on Earth.

To learn more, follow the timeline through this book to trace the history of long-distance communication technologies from the earliest civilizations to the present day. Another volume in this series charts writing and printing developments through time.

Chapter 1

Communication in Ancient Times
2300's B.C.—A.D. 120's

In ancient times, people first communicated using the spoken word. **Couriers,** whether running or on horseback, carried messages over longer distances. People also used drumbeats, fire, and smoke signals to send simple messages by sound and sight. These methods sent coded messages. Each signal represented the letters or ideas in a message. A person had to *decode* (translate) the signals to understand what they meant. For example, a person might hear three drumbeats and understand that those sounds meant "enemy approaching."

2300's B.C.

People have long used pigeons to carry messages. Certain pigeons tend to fly straight home. These homing pigeons can fly for hundreds of miles or kilometers. Sargon of Akkad, a ruler in Mesopotamia (in what is now Iraq) who ruled from 2334 B.C.-2279 B.C., ordered his messengers to travel with homing pigeons. If the messenger was attacked, he would release the pigeon. Ancient Egyptians, Persians, and Greeks also used homing pigeons.

c. 1750 B.C.

King Hammurabi (?-1750 B.C.) of Babylonia (in what is now southern Iraq) used a courier system for messages.

c. 1203 B.C.

Pharaoh Merneptah of Egypt, who ruled from about 1213 B.C. to 1203 B.C., asked his men to keep logs of couriers who passed through kingdom guard posts.

However, such signals could not travel farther than people could see or hear. The ancient Greeks solved this problem by creating a **visual telegraph.** They built a number of tall brick walls over a distance of land. Each wall could be seen from the next one. To send a message, a person standing on one wall would light fires at particular positions on that wall. The position of the fires on the wall represented the words of the message. A person standing on the next wall a short distance away watched for the fires on the first wall. Then, the watcher lit the same fires on his wall. These fires sent the message to the person on the next wall. This watching and fire-lighting system continued as far as the walls were built over the land. In this way, messages could be relayed, or sent, over very long distances.

Greek historian and soldier Xenophon (430? B.C.-355? B.C.) wrote of using sunlight to send messages. During a war between the ancient Greek cities of Athens and Sparta, Spartan soldiers used a polished shield to send sun signals. The shiny shield reflected sunlight. When the soldiers flashed the shield in certain directions and at different speeds, the sun signs formed coded messages. This signaling method is called *heliographic messaging*.

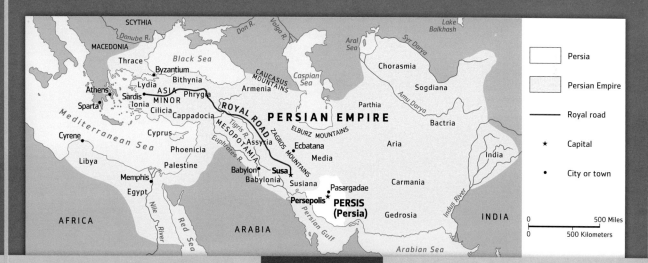

c. 405 B.C.

400's B.C.

Writing in the 400's B.C., Greek historian Herodotus (484? B.C.-425? B.C.) described a special type of mail system in ancient Persia. Throughout the Persian Empire, in areas of what is now Afghanistan and Iran, messengers carried, delivered, and picked up mail across the land. Couriers traveled the Royal Road by horseback or walking. The Royal Road stretched some 1,600 miles (2,600 kilometers) from ancient Persia to the Mediterranean Sea. The road connected most of the major cities of the empire.

Communication in Ancient Times

2300's B.C.—A.D. 120's

The ancient Greeks and Persians both founded large societies. Long-range communication was important to both civilizations. The ancient Romans eventually conquered ancient Greece. They created an even bigger empire. At its height, the Roman Empire covered about half of Europe, North Africa, and parts of the Middle East.

To send messages across such a large territory, the ancient Romans created a well-organized postal system called the *cursus publicus*. A postal system collects, handles, and delivers letters, messages, and packages. The Romans built relay

Hannibal (247 B.C.-183 B.C.), the greatest general and statesman of Carthage, an ancient North African city, used smoke signals to plan an invasion of Roman territory during the Second Punic War (218 B.C.-201 B.C.).

The Mauryan Empire covered much of what is now India and Pakistan. The empire lasted from around 324 B.C. to 185 B.C. The Mauryans built a network of roads, public wells, rest houses, and a mail service.

210's B.C.

200's B.C.

stations on the empire's major roadways. These stations were spaced the same distance from one another along the road. At these stations, messengers were able to rest, pick up and drop off mail, and select new horses to ride. Using these stations, messengers were able to travel between 41 and 64 miles (66 and 103 kilometers) per day.

For military communications, ancient Romans and their enemies continued to use many types of visual signaling systems. The Romans used tall fire beacons, lit torches, and flag signals to communicate between forts. Though these signals were useful, they only sent messages as far as the eye could see.

Ancient Roman emperor Hadrian (A.D. 76–A.D. 138) built a wall across what is now northern Great Britain to mark the northern boundary of the Roman Empire. This wall also helped prevent enemy attacks. Towers and forts were built at regular points along the wall. People used flag signals to communicate long distances between the towers and forts along the wall. They used two groups of five flags each. The number of flags raised represented a letter of the alphabet. They continued to raise different groupings of flags until all of the words in a message were spelled out.

A.D. 120's

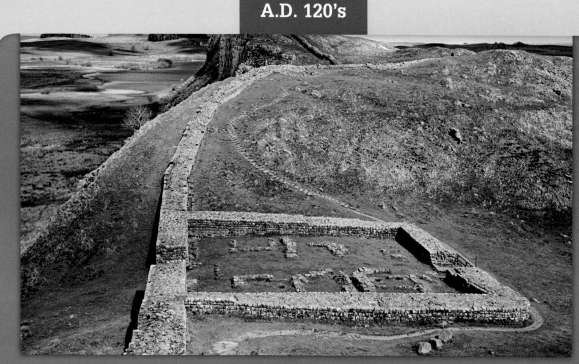

A Timeline of Long-Distance Communication

Chapter 2

Communication Systems Advance
A.D. 800's—Mid-1400's

During the **Middle Ages,** long-distance communication methods remained mostly the same. European kings and nobles communicated through private **couriers.** But most people could not read or write. They heard news from public announcements or wandering singers and poets. By the A.D. 1100's in Europe, knights and nobles began using a new form of visual communication called *heraldry*. They wore decorative symbols to signal their identities.

A.D. 800's

The Byzantine Empire constructed an extensive beacon signaling system. These beacons were large brick platforms or towers. Huge bonfires could be lit on the top of the tower. The beacons were built on hilltops within eyesight view of each other. When the fires were lit, the beacon system provided early warning of an oncoming enemy attack. This system stretched from the empire's east to the capital of Constantinople, now called Istanbul, in modern-day Turkey.

10

In the late A.D. 400's, the Western Roman Empire fell. The remaining Eastern Roman Empire developed into the Byzantine Empire. The Byzantine Empire centered on the Mediterranean, hugging the coasts of Africa, Asia, and Europe, with its capital of Constantinople (now the city of Istanbul). In the Middle Ages, the *cursus publicus* postal system continued operation in parts of the Byzantine Empire. The decline of the Roman road network and the break-up of Europe into individual states eventually caused the mail service to disappear in the early A.D. 800's.

During the A.D. 600's and A.D. 700's in the Middle East, the Islamic Empire used a postal system. During China's Tang dynasty (A.D. 618-A.D. 907), a network of more than 1,600 postal stations stretched across the Chinese empire.

Identifying symbols, called *coats of arms,* first appeared during the Crusades. The Crusades were Christian military expeditions that lasted from the late A.D. 1000's to the late A.D. 1300's. Crusaders, called Christian knights, wore coats of arms on their flags and shields. The symbols helped soldiers to recognize friend from enemy on the battlefield. They also showed where the king or lord was located during battle. Coats of arms also indicated who was of noble rank, or position, in society. The coat of arms developed into a larger communication system called *heraldry.*

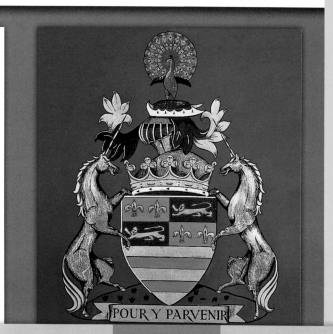

POUR Y PARVENIR

c. A.D. 1100's

A.D. 1200's

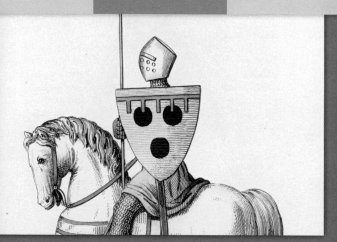

By the A.D. 1200's, noble families used symbols of heraldry to identify themselves outside of battle. Each coat of arms was unique to a certain family. They included such colorful decorations as animals, flowers, and shapes. People also placed their coat of arms on clothing and other possessions.

Communication Systems Advance
A.D. 800's—Mid-1400's

In China, long-range communication systems had been established for some time. Under the Song dynasty, from A.D. 960 to 1279, mail service was ranked according to price. To send a letter through the postal system, people had to pay a special fee. Messengers rode horses and delivered the letters according to the price paid. The higher the price paid for the letter, the faster the letter was delivered.

In the 1200's, Italian traveler Marco Polo visited China. He saw an organized postal system run by the Mongol Emperor Kublai Khan (1215-1294). Khan's capital was called Cambaluc, located in today's city of Beijing in China. According to Polo,

Italian Marco Polo (1254-1324?) wrote a now-famous book entitled *The Description of the World* about his travels through Asia. He described a large postal system, which consisted of a vast network of **courier** stations. A later edition of this book is called *The Travels of Marco Polo.*

The *Black Book of the Admiralty*, published around 1338, is the earliest surviving book to mention English naval flag signals. The English navy used two flag signals to communicate between ships. When one flag was raised, it notified the captains of each ship to come aboard the admiral's ship for a meeting. The other flag signaled a sighting of the enemy.

1298

c. 1338

many roadways were built out from the center of the capital city. The roadways led in all directions. Along these roads, postal system relay stations were located about every 25 miles (40 kilometers). Polo wrote that mail messengers could ride on horseback up to 200 miles (320 kilometers) per day. At relay stations, messengers traded tired horses for rested ones. The messengers used horns to announce their arrival at the stations so that new horses could be readied to ride. Like those of the ancient Roman postal system, these relay stations allowed the messengers a chance to rest, eat, and drop off or collect new letters or packages. Then, the rider continued on his journey with a fresh horse.

1400's

The Inca created an enormous empire in the mountains of South America. The Inca Empire included parts of present-day Colombia, Ecuador, Peru, Bolivia, Chile, and Argentina. They built a network of roads to link the empire together. To communicate over long distances, the Inca used a relay system of foot messengers called *chasquis*. Small huts were built every mile (1.6 kilometers) along the roads. In each hut, a chasqui messenger waited and watched for another chasqui to run near the hut. When he spotted a messenger running, the second chasqui came out of his hut and ran alongside the first messenger. As they ran, the message was passed from person to person. Then, the second chasqui ran alone to the next hut along the route. The second chasqui passed on the message to a third chasqui, and so on. Using this running relay method, a message could travel about 150 miles (240 kilometers) in one day.

1468?

Death of German printer and inventor Johannes Gutenberg (b. 1395?).

Chapter 3

From Printing to Telegraphs
Late 1400's—1870

In the 1400's, a German inventor named Johannes Gutenberg introduced his printing press to Europe. Soon, printed books were common. More people learned to read and write. With the printing press, new knowledge spread quickly.

Gutenberg's invention helped make written texts available to everyone. But it did not significantly change the ways people communicated over long distances. In the 1500's, 1600's, and 1700's, people sent long-range messages in the same way as

King Charles I (1600-1649) was the first English monarch to offer mail services to the public.

Merchant William Dockwra (1635-1716) organized the London Penny Post. This service delivered mail anywhere in London for the price of one penny. Letters were prepaid and marked with a stamp. Letter deliveries were made almost hourly. Dockwra introduced the practice of postmarking letters to indicate when and where they had been mailed. His system worked much better than other postal services. It was so successful that the British government took it over in 1682.

1516   **1635**   **1673**   **1680**

King Henry VIII (1491-1547) of England appointed a Master of the Posts. Later, the Master of the Posts began to organize a regular postal service schedule along the major roads leading to and from London.

In the British colonies in North America, New York colony Governor Francis Lovelace (1621-1675) established a monthly postal service between New York City and Boston.

14

they did in ancient times. Because many people were now able to read and write, more and more people sent letters to one another. The increase in mailed letters meant that new postal systems were developed. These systems made sending letters easier. New ships could also carry letters farther and faster by water.

In France, a new **visual telegraph** system improved upon the early system used by the ancient Greeks. But most messages only traveled as fast as horses and ships could carry them.

By the mid-1780's, stagecoaches, or horse-drawn carriages, were first used to deliver mail and packages in Great Britain. These coaches quickly replaced messengers on horseback and greatly improved the efficiency of the service.

French inventor Claude Chappe (1763-1805) developed the **semaphore optical telegraph.** Chappe built 15 tower stations on hilltops stretching 130 miles (210 kilometers) between the cities of Paris and Lille, France. A tower stood at each station, holding wooden crossbeams. The beams had winglike parts on each end. The operators could change the angle of the beams and wings in hundreds of different ways. Each combination of beams and wings represented a letter, number, or word. People at the next tower observed the messages with telescopes. They then used the beams and wings at their station to pass the message farther along the route.

1794

From Printing to Telegraphs
Late 1400's—1870

In the early 1800's, the **semaphore optical telegraph** was the most advanced form of long-distance communication. During the Napoleonic Wars in Europe (1796 to 1815), the semaphore was heavily used for military communications in France. Similar messaging systems were developed in Great Britain, Sweden, and the United States. Under ideal conditions, messages could be relayed at speeds of up to 120 miles (192 kilometers) per hour using this telegraph method. But this system had some disadvantages. The towers could not be kept secret, so both armies could see the same messages. Also, people made errors when positioning beams and wings, so incorrect messages sometimes were sent.

In the early 1800's, American shipowners offered a new type of transatlantic service called *packet ships.* These large ships carried mail packets, cargo, and passengers across the Atlantic Ocean from North America to Europe. These ships sailed on regular schedules. Before this time, ships sailed only if they had a full load of cargo and passengers. In 1818, regular packet ship service began sailing between New York City and Liverpool, England.

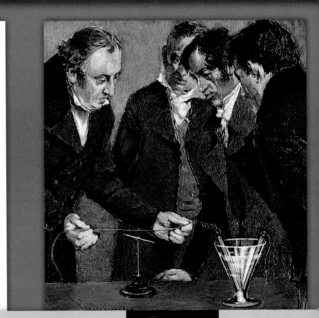

1818

1820

Danish physicist Hans Christian Oersted (1777-1851) discovered that an electric current will cause a magnetized metal needle to move. The discovery of the relationship between electric currents and magnetism laid the groundwork for the invention of the **telegraph.**

In the 1800's, communication suddenly sped up because scientists learned how to control and use electricity and magnetism. Magnetism is a force that causes magnets and certain other objects to attract or *repel* (push away from) each other. Scientists discovered how to use magnets to control **electric currents**, or flows of electrically charged particles. The scientists were able to move currents through metal wires to power electric devices. Electric currents move fast—at nearly the speed of light.

Eventually, people learned how to send coded signals, or messages, using these electric currents and wires. People also started laying longer and longer wires to connect distant locations. These developments paved the way for a much better form of long-range communication—the electric telegraph.

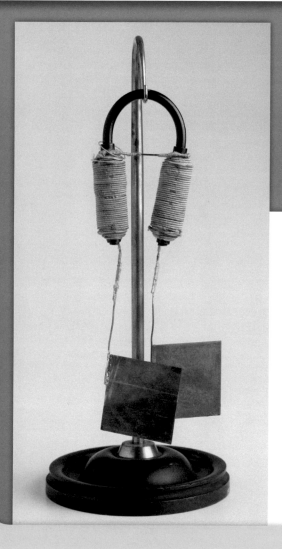

American physicist Joseph Henry (1797-1878) sent an electric current over 1 mile (1.6 kilometers) of wire to activate, or turn on, an electromagnet.

1830

Another step towards the creation of the telegraph was the invention of the **electromagnet** (left) by British scientist William Sturgeon (1783-1850). An electromagnet typically contains a core of iron surrounded by a coil of wire. When an electric current is passed through the wire, the iron core becomes a powerful magnet. American Joseph Henry improved Sturgeon's design a few years later.

1825

From Printing to Telegraphs
Late 1400's—1870

American inventor Samuel F. B. Morse invented the electric **telegraph** in 1837. With the electric telegraph, people could send a coded message along a metal wire. A person at one end of the wire sent the message by varying the **electric current** moving through the wire. At the other end of the wire, another person could *decode* (translate) the message by using an **electromagnet** to show the variations in the current. These variations stood for different letters or numbers. When put together, the variations created a message. This communication system came to be called *Morse code,* named after Samuel Morse.

American inventor Samuel F. B. Morse (1791-1872) and his assistant Alfred Vail (1807-1859) used Joseph Henry's invention of the electromagnet to design a successful telegraph system. They also developed a system for sending messages called *Morse code.* Morse code has two symbols—a "dot" and a "dash." To send Morse code, a telegraph operator presses a switch so that a current flows through a telegraph wire. Tapping the switch means "dot." Holding the switch a bit longer means "dash." On the other end of the line, someone translates the pattern of dots and dashes sent through the wires. Certain patterns of dots and dashes stand for certain letters or numbers.

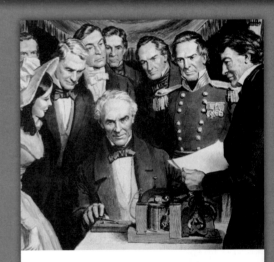

The electric telegraph was used for the first time to transmit a news story in the United States. Afterward, news reporters used the telegraph to send stories to their newspaper offices.

1844

1837

1840

The British postal service started using stamps. Placing a stamp on a letter showed that the fee for the letter's delivery was already paid. Before stamps, the person receiving a letter usually paid the mail carrier.

During the 1840's, the telegraph became the most important method of long-distance communication. By the 1850's, many countries around the world had developed a telegraph system.

At the same time, sending handwritten letters continued to become easier and faster. The British developed a postage-stamp system. In the United States, the Pony Express offered quick delivery of letters across the continent. But the Pony Express was very expensive. It was used by newspapers and businessmen, but not used much by people writing private letters. It was not nearly as fast as the telegraph. The transcontinental telegraph, a system of wires that stretched from the eastern portion of North America to the western end, opened on October 24, 1861. The Pony Express closed two days later.

The Pony Express was a mail delivery service that operated in the United States between the states of Missouri and California. Pony Express messengers rode horses or ponies and carried saddlebags of mail across the 1,966-mile (3,146-kilometer) trail. The service had 190 stations along the trail, 80 riders, and about 400 horses. This service allowed faster communication between the eastern and western areas of the United States. But, the Pony Express only lasted 18 months and closed just after the completion of the transcontinental telegraph system.

1860

1866

The first successful transatlantic telegraph cable was laid. The cable was laid underwater in the Atlantic Ocean to connect Valentia, Ireland, to Heart's Content, a city in Newfoundland, Canada.

Chapter 4

Speech, Over Wires and Through the Air
1875—1915

In the 1870's, centrally located **telegraph** offices existed in most major cities in the United States and Europe. The telegraph used electricity to transmit coded messages along a wire. Though the telegraph successfully sent messages over long distances, some scientists wondered if human speech and sounds could also be sent over the same wires from one location to another.

1875

Scottish-born teacher Alexander Graham Bell (1847-1922) and his assistant, American Thomas Watson (1854-1934), experimented with the harmonic telegraph. The device sent several telegraph messages at the same time over a single wire. During their experiments in the U.S., in 1875, one of the device's metal reeds became stuck. When Watson plucked the reed to loosen it, Bell heard the sound in another room through his **receiver.** Bell realized he'd just sent sound over a wire.

The next year, Bell was testing a new **transmitter.** He said, "Mr. Watson, come here. I want you!" Watson, in another room, heard every word. For the first time, speech had been sent over a wire.

In June 1876, Bell demonstrated his telephone at the Centennial Exposition in Philadelphia, Pennsylvania. In October, Bell and Watson held the first long-distance conversation over the telephone. They spoke between Boston and Cambridgeport, a part of Cambridge, Massachusetts, a distance of about 2 miles (3 kilometers).

The first working telephone was invented by Alexander Graham Bell, a Scottish-born teacher living in the United States. The machine turns sounds from one end of the wire into electrical signals, and then back into sounds again on the other end of the wire. Later, Bell and a group of investors opened the Bell Telephone Company. This company charged a fee for people to use the telephone service to communicate with others. Another company, Western Union Telegraph, set up a competing telephone business. However, Bell held a **patent** for his invention and had a right to operate the only telephone business.

The telephone revolutionized long-distance communications, also called *telecommunications,* even more than the telegraph. But just like the telegraph, telephone messages needed to travel over wires.

The first **switchboard** began operation in Boston. A switchboard helps connect all of the phone lines in a certain area. When a person wanted to make a phone call, they called the switchboard operator to connect their call with another person. The operator "switched" the phone call by manually plugging electric cords into a switchboard.

1877

1877

1878

American inventor Thomas Edison (1847-1931) created the phonograph. The phonograph, also called a *record player,* is a device that records and reproduces sounds. Until the mid-1980's record players were the most common device for listening to music and sound recordings.

The Bell Telephone Company sued Western Union Telegraph over its competing telephone businesses. In 1879, Western Union recognized Bell's patents and sold its telephone business to Bell's company.

Speech, Over Wires and Through the Air
1875—1915

During the 1880's and 1890's, the telephone became one of the most important forms of long-distance communication. In 1885, the American Telephone and Telegraph Company (AT&T) was founded to operate the long-distance telephone network. By that time, telephone lines connected every major American city.

In the 1890's, a completely new form of telecommunication was developed— radio. **Telegraphs** and telephones relied on wires to carry their signals, so the sender and the recipient needed to be connected by the wires.

1888

German physicist Heinrich Hertz (1857-1894) performed experiments that proved electromagnetic waves exist. Electromagnetic waves are also known as electromagnetic radiation. Hertz discovered that radio waves, a form of electromagnetic radiation, traveled in straight lines through the air.

1879

1891

Nikola Tesla (1856-1943), an American inventor from Austria-Hungary, created the Tesla coil. This device can change the *voltage* (flow) of certain electric currents. These currents could be tuned, or adjusted, to create a certain pattern of sound waves. In the process, the device could send out powerful radio waves with the same pattern. The Tesla coil became an essential part of radio **transmitters** still used today.

Death of Scottish physicist James Clerk Maxwell (b. 1831).

By contrast, radio signals passed through the air. The new invention untied long-range communication from wires altogether. Radio allowed quick communication between any two points on land, at sea, or in the sky.

The invention of the radio began in the 1830's. While experimenting with **electromagnets,** scientists discovered that an **electric current** in one wire could produce a current in another unconnected wire. This discovery puzzled the scientists. In 1864, Scottish physicist James Clerk Maxwell explained this phenomenon by suggesting there are **electromagnetic waves** that travel through space. The light we see is made of electromagnetic waves. But other types of electromagnetic waves—like radio waves—are invisible. Detecting electromagnetic waves was an important step for developing radio communication.

American inventor Almon Strowger (1839-1902) **patented** a system that connected calls automatically without the need for a telephone **switchboard** and operators.

In 1895, Italian physicist Guglielmo Marconi (1874-1937) used radio waves to create wireless telegraphy—or radio. Wireless telegraphy did not need wires to send messages. Instead, telegraph signals were sent through the air using radio waves. Marconi repeated Hertz's experiments. He found that when his **transmitter** and **receiver** were connected to the ground, and when he used a tall **antenna,** he could greatly increase a signal's range to reach far distances. Marconi's radio transmitter changed Morse code signals into radio waves. Then, the radio receiver changed the waves back into signals. Marconi shared the 1909 Nobel prize in physics for his work.

1891

1895

Speech, Over Wires and Through the Air
1875—1915

By the early 1900's many people and businesses were switching from using the **telegraph** to using the telephone for both short- and long-distance communication. To use a telegraph, trained operators were needed to translate messages into and out of Morse code. But, with the telephone, one person simply spoke to another over the wires.

In 1899, British inventor Donald Murray (1865-1945) filed a **patent** for the teletypewriter system. This system used a keyboard to send typed messages and a printer to receive the text. These written telegraph messages are called

Canadian-born physicist Reginald Fessenden (1866-1932) made possibly the first transmission of human speech over radio waves, across a distance of about 1 mile (1.6 kilometers). Fessenden invented a radio system that produced a powerful wave, called a *carrier wave.* By adding a sound signal (called *amplitude modulation,* or *AM*) to this wave, he could send speech and music from a **transmitter** to a **receiver.**

1900

1904

British engineer Sir John Fleming (1849-1945) invented a **vacuum tube** to better detect radio signals. A vacuum tube is an **electronic** device. It is an airless container, or vacuum, with a glass shell. Electronic signals travel better through such a vacuum. Earlier inventors had experimented with vacuum tubes. Fleming's was the first that worked well for radios. Vacuum tubes were later used in televisions and electronic computers.

Movie theaters, known as *nickelodeons,* started opening across the United States. They quickly become a popular form of mass communication.

1904

1905

Over three million telephones were in use in the United States.

telegrams. Telegrams were sent using the same wires as telegraphs. The telegram was received at a central office and delivered by a messenger to the intended reader. Sometimes, the messenger even sang the telegram's words to the recipient.

In the early 1900's, several technological breakthroughs happened in the field of radio. Marconi transmitted radio signals across the Atlantic Ocean. Reginald Fessenden, a Canadian-born American physicist, pioneered speech over the radio waves. These achievements helped develop radio and **broadcasting** during the first half of the 1900's. At first, radio found a practical use in ship-to-ship and ship-to-shore communication. This new connection among ships and others on land helped to save thousands of lives in shipwrecks and other disasters at sea. However, the most significant role for radio came to be one-way, **mass communication.**

American inventor Lee De Forest (1873-1961) invented a new vacuum tube that made radio signals much stronger. With his invention, radio signals could be heard through a speaker.

1906

Two ships, the S.S. *Republic* and the S.S. *Florida*, collided with each other in the Atlantic Ocean. During the disaster, the *Republic* made the first-ever radio distress call that brought rescuers to the scene. This call for help resulted in saving around 1,200 lives.

1909

The world's first airmail service began in Great Britain between the towns of Hendon and Windsor.

1911   **1915**

A transcontinental phone service began between New York City and San Francisco in the United States.

Chapter 5

Broadcasting Communication
1920—Early 1960's

In the 1920's, many new radio stations began **broadcasting** to the public. Soon, millions of people both short and long distances away from the stations tuned in to the radio. They listened to live music, news reports, and drama or comedy shows. Because of its popularity, radio technology continued to improve during the 1930's and 1940's. From the 1920's to the early 1950's, radio served as the main source of information and entertainment for many people. This time is known as the Golden Age of Radio Broadcasting.

Russian-born American inventor Vladimir Zworykin (1889-1982) developed the *iconoscope*. The iconoscope was a TV camera tube that produced good-quality pictures. He also developed the *kinescope*, a picture tube used in TV sets for receiving images.

Scottish engineer John Logie Baird (1888-1946) revealed the first complete television system. Baird's system used mechanical devices in the camera and television **receiver.** This system used a rotating disk that broke the full image into smaller pieces and produced a flickering image on the screen.

1923

1925

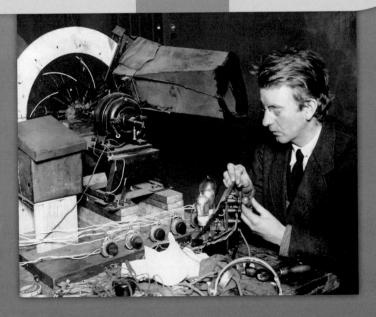

Meanwhile, scientists were developing another form of broadcasting communication, the television. Since the 1800's, scientists wondered how images could be transmitted using an electrical device. It took many advances in technology to make such an idea feasible. Scottish engineer John Logie Baird demonstrated the first complete television system in 1925. Television signals were sent with radio waves. In a radio, the waves simply encode such sounds as voice and music. In a television, radio waves encode voices, music, and pictures. Baird's system produced basic, fuzzy images in black and white. Later inventors improved on Baird's design. Other technological advances also helped the quality of TV pictures to improve.

1929

Zworykin displayed the first **electronic** television system. Instead of using a spinning disk, the electronic television system used a special tube that transformed video (image) signals into patterns of light. These light patterns reproduced the scene in front of the camera directly onto the television screen.

American engineer Edwin Armstrong (1890-1954) invented frequency modulation (FM), which gave a clearer radio signal than AM.

One of the first televised events was the 1936 Summer Olympic Games held in Berlin, Germany. Few people owned personal televisions, so they gathered to watch the event on TV's in department stores and theaters.

1933

1933

1936

On March 12, 1933, United States President Franklin Delano Roosevelt (1882-1945) gave his first of 31 radio talks to the American public. These "fireside chats" allowed Roosevelt to describe government policies directly to the people. His effective use of radio demonstrated the great force of **mass communication.**

Broadcasting Communication
1920—Early 1960's

The Golden Age of Radio Broadcasting ended during the mid-1950's. At this time, television emerged as the leading provider of **broadcast** information and entertainment. In the 1930's, the first TV companies were set up. The TV stations broadcast many types of programs, including situation comedies and cartoons.

The television is one of the most important forms of both short- and long-distance communication. In 1945, there were only 7,000 TV sets in the United States. But, **mass communication** by television boomed after World War II (1939-1945). By 1950, there were over 12 million TV's in American homes and businesses.

1953

1956

Undersea telephone cables linked North America and Europe.

Color TV broadcasting began in the United States.

Three American physicists—(pictured left to right) John Bardeen (1908-1991), William Shockley (1910-1989), and Walter H. Brattain (1902-1987)—invented the **transistor.** It replaced bulky **vacuum tubes** in such **electronic** devices as radios and TV's. Radios with transistors were much smaller and easier to carry. Transistors also became an important part of electronic computers.

1947

The popularity of TV led to improvements in picture and sound quality. In the 1950's, television programs were broadcast in color for the first time. Programs could be recorded on videotape. Videotape is a wide, magnetized tape with tracks for recording and reproducing both images and sounds. Before this time, all transmitted TV programs were live productions or made from film. Unlike film, which needs to be developed, videotape could be played back immediately after recording. Early TV screens measured 7 or 10 inches (18 or 25 centimeters) diagonally. By the 1960's, many people owned 27-inch (69-centimeter) screens.

In the late 1950's the first artificial communications satellites were launched into orbit around Earth by the United States. In outer space, a communications satellite can bounce wireless signals among distant points on Earth's surface.

The United States launched the first communications satellite, named SCORE (Signal Communications by Orbiting Relay Equipment). It could bounce radio signals back to Earth. It was the first satellite to relay voice messages from one location to another.

1958

1961

Stereophonic (stereo) FM radio broadcasting began. In stereo, different sounds come out of the left and right **receivers** called *speakers*. This stereo method makes music sound richer and more natural, as if hearing it live.

Chapter 6

Digital Communication
Late 1960's—2005

Since the 1950's, the world has become a more connected place thanks to improvements in telecommunication. In radio and television **broadcasts,** information takes the form of **electromagnetic waves.** Modern computers, on the other hand, do not encode information in waves. Instead, they use patterns of numbers—the digits 1 and 0—to stand for words, sounds, images, and videos. This is called **digital** communication. The word *digital* means *using information in the form of numbers*.

In the 1960's, the United States and the Soviet Union were close to fighting a nuclear war. The U.S. government worried that a Soviet attack could wreck the country's phone lines and prevent important governmental communication, so they created ARPANet. On this network, messages are split into "packets" of **electronic** signals. These packets are not sent and received in a direct line, like phone calls. Instead, each packet can travel through the network along any available path. ARPANet eventually became the modern Internet.

The first small home computer, the Altair, went on sale to the public. The computer was sold as a kit for people to assemble at home. But the public did not yet have access to the Internet.

Late 1960's | 1973 | 1975

American Martin Cooper (1928-   ), working for Motorola, demonstrated the first mobile cellular telephone. Cellular phones did not need wires to work. They sent and received voice calls with radio signals. The signals travel between the phone's **antenna** and cellular towers called *base stations*. Each base station covers a small area called a *cell*.

Computers had been in development since the 1820's. Early working computers of the 1950's were massive, expensive machines used by factories, businesses, and governments. They did not yet allow people to communicate with one another. As technology advanced, computers became smaller and more powerful. New forms of communication arose as the world's computers became linked on the Internet.

In 1969, the development of the Internet began with a project called *ARPANet*. The Advanced Research Projects Agency (ARPA), part of the U.S. Department of Defense, funded the research project. It linked military and scientific computer systems across the country. Later, part of ARPANet became the Internet. Within decades, digital computers connected to the Internet had become major tools for long-distance communication.

Japan introduced the first commercial cellular telephone system.

A telephone system began operating between New York City and Washington, D.C., using **optical fibers** rather than traditional metal cables. An optical fiber is a thin glass thread. Laser light travels through the thread. The pattern of laser flashes forms a digital code. Optical fibers can transmit much more information than older wire telephone lines.

1979   **1981**   **1983**

Over 200 computers in the United States were linked to ARPANet by 1981. ARPANet was split into two parts. One part was used by the military. The second part was taken over by the National Science Foundation (NSF). The NSF combined ARPANet with its own National Science Foundation Network (NSFNET). The new NSFNET eventually became the Internet.

Digital Communication
Late 1960's—2005

The 1980's and early 1990's witnessed the beginning of the Internet and the World Wide Web. This technological progress enabled the widespread use of **digital** communication technology. Digital systems provide stronger and clearer signals than those encoded in **electromagnetic waves.**

In 1991, British computer scientist Tim Berners-Lee developed a system, called the *World Wide Web*, that would turn the Internet into a tool that anyone could use. The Web is not the same as the Internet. Web pages, or websites, are stored on Internet-connected computers. A website contains hypertext. Hypertext can link

Facsimile, or fax, machines became a popular way for businesses to send printed material over telephone lines. A fax machine made a copy, or facsimile, of the original document and sent the copy directly to another fax machine.

Lighter, smaller digital cell phones became available to consumers. A popular feature of the new phones was short messaging service (SMS). SMS allowed people to send brief text, rather than spoken, messages to another cell phone.

1987

1991

1992

British scientist Tim Berners-Lee (1955-) developed the World Wide Web. The Web made it easy to use the Internet from a personal computer. Berners-Lee created Hypertext Markup Language (HTML), which is used to write web page files. He also created Hypertext Transfer Protocol (HTTP), a set of rules for linking words and pages together.

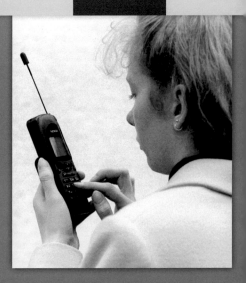

one website directly with other websites. These linked web pages, all together, form the World Wide Web. Web browsers and search engines soon appeared, making it much easier to search for information on the Web.

Through computers and mobile devices, the Web changed the way people communicate over both short and long distances. The Internet and Web made it easier to connect with one another on a daily basis. People sent the first e-mails, or **electronic** mail, as early as the 1960's. But it took the personal computer and the Web to make this communication method popular. Sending letters through the post office could take days. Sending an e-mail took minutes or less. Later, instant messaging programs enabled even quicker written communication than e-mail.

Digital audio **broadcasting** (DAB) was introduced at a world conference in Spain. It offered better sound quality than non-digital radio. Satellite radio is a form of DAB.

1992

Mid-1990's

1996

By the mid-1990's, millions of individuals, businesses, and schools owned personal electronic computers. Many devices were easy-to-use desktop computers connected by cables to the Internet. Using both a computer and the Internet, people could quickly send messages to one another using e-mail services. Later, portable laptop, or notebook, computers became as popular as desktop computers.

The first popular instant messaging (IM) program, ICQ, launched. With an IM program, people can communicate with typed messages directly over the Internet. IM is faster and simpler than sending e-mails. In the following years, other Internet companies, including America Online (AOL)®, Yahoo!®, and Google™, launched their own IM services.

Digital Communication
Late 1960's—2005

During the late 1990's and early 2000's, the Internet became the world's most important communication system for work, leisure, entertainment, and business. Several technological improvements to the Internet service made this possible.

At first, people needed to "dial-up" to connect to the Internet. "Dial-up" service used wire telephone lines to connect a computer to the Internet. This service tended to be very slow. Broadband connections, introduced in the 1990's, transfer data much faster than do dial-up connections. Faster connections meant people could easily send and receive videos and similar large digital files of information.

2003

The social networking sites Friendster® and MySpace® launched online. The networks let people create web pages called *profiles*. Then they could find the profiles of their friends and family. Once the profiles were connected, people could keep in touch by writing messages to one another through the web page. Eventually, social networks became an important form of quick communication. Users can post updates, or messages that are instantly seen by everyone with whom they are connected.

1999

Blogger™ and LiveJournal™, two popular public blogging services, launched.

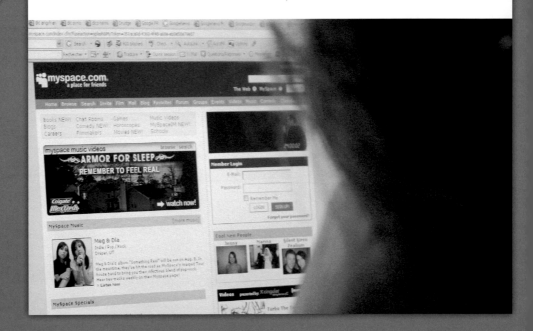

In the late 1990's, wireless Internet access, or Wi-Fi, was introduced. Wi-Fi allows people to connect to the Internet using radio signals instead of wire cables. This technology laid the groundwork for such mobile devices as smartphones and tablet computers, which wirelessly connect to the Internet.

During the 1990's, websites were mainly built and run by computer experts with little involvement from Internet users. But in the early 2000's, the Internet became much more interactive. This increased interactivity became known as Web 2.0. Any person could post content on *blogs* (short for web logs). On websites called social networks, people could easily connect with friends and family. With Web 2.0, people found many new ways to communicate.

The BlackBerry®, one of the first popular smartphones, was launched. People could easily send and receive e-mails on their BlackBerries over a cellular network.

2003

Facebook®, which became the most popular social network, was created.

2003

2004   **2005**

Skype™, a computer application offering video chat and voice calls, launched.

YouTube™, the video-sharing website, launched.

Chapter 7

A Connected World
2006—Today

Since the early 2000's, the Internet has only increased in popularity. New types of technology allow people to communicate in many ways. People no longer simply speak to each other in person or over the phone. Today, they share photos, videos, games, texts, and music. People can use laptop computers, smartphones, tablet computers, and even wristwatches to remain connected to the Internet at all times of the day. At the same time, many people have stopped using such older communication technologies as fax machines and wire-connected telephones.

Twitter™, the social networking site, was launched. Users could post short messages called *tweets*. Users could easily post tweets from cell phones.

Steve Jobs (1955-2011), cofounder of Apple, Inc., with Steve Wozniak (1950-   ), helped to develop the iPhone®. This smartphone combined a wireless phone, a music and video player, and mobile Internet and e-mail capabilities.

2006

2007

Not only has communication between individuals increased, interactions among groups of people has also grown. No matter where a person is in the world, he or she can use the Internet to connect with a network of friends. Such social networking sites as Facebook® and Twitter™ allow users to share information about their lives. Social networks also help to form communities of likeminded people, to raise awareness of global issues, and to fight for political change.

In the future, advances in communication technology likely will change the devices on which we send messages. Still, people will continue to relay information to one another as the world becomes an even more connected place of communication.

The United States government classified Internet service providers as *common carriers*. On a common carrier, all communications must be treated the same as they travel over the network. The classification helps ensure that data transmitted over the Internet receives equal treatment regardless of its sender—a concept called *net neutrality*.

2009

2015   **2015**

Between 2009 and 2013, many countries around the world made the switch to **broadcasting** only **digital** television. With this change, digital television signals were broadcast in high-definition (HD). HD television produces extremely sharp, colorful images on the screen.

Apple, Inc. released the Apple Watch®, a *smartwatch* that links to a user's iPhone to enable communication from the wrist.

Glossary

antenna   a rod or wire that sends or receives electromagnetic waves.

broadcast   (n.) a message sent out by radio or television; a radio or television program of speech, music, or the like; (v.) to send out programs by radio or television to a large audience at one time.

courier   a special messenger who carries information from one location to another.

digital   a system that converts signals or information into a series of the numerals 0 and 1. This numerical code is the language used by computers.

electric current   the movement or flow of electric charges.

electromagnet   a temporary magnet formed when electric current flows through a wire or other conductor.

electromagnetic waves   related patterns of electric and magnetic forces that travel through space, including visible light, radio waves, and X rays.

electronic   using patterns in electric currents to carry signals.

mass communication   any form of communication (such as newspapers, radio, or television) that reaches large numbers of people.

Middle Ages   the period in European history between ancient and modern times, from about the A.D. 400's through about the 1400's. The end date depends on the region of Europe considered.

optical fiber   a thin glass thread through which light signals can be sent.

patent   a government-issued document that gives an inventor exclusive rights to make, use, and sell an invention for a limited time.

receiver   a device that detects broadcast signals and converts them into a form people can see, hear, or otherwise use.

semaphore   a method of signaling with targets or flags. Each flag or target position has a meaning that is read by those trained in semaphore. The **semaphore optical telegraph** is an example of this system.

stereophonic   electronic equipment that reproduces lifelike sounds using at least two speakers. Also called *stereo*.

switchboard   a central location where telephone lines are connected and controlled.

telegram   a message sent by telegraph and delivered in written or printed form.

telegraph   a device used to send messages by means of wires and electric currents.

transistor   a device that controls the flow of electric current in radios, television sets, computers, and other electronic equipment.

transmitter   a device that sends out an electrical signal. The signals that can encode messages, sounds, voices, or other types of information.

vacuum tube   a sealed glass tube from which almost all of the air has been removed.

visual telegraph   a signaling device or system used to send messages by sight.

Find Out More

Books

Cell Phone Science: What Happens When You Call and Why by Michele Sequeira and Michael Westphal (University of New Mexico Press, 2010)

How Does a Network Work? by Matt Anniss (Gareth Stevens Publishing, 2014)

Larry Page and Sergey Brin: Information at Your Fingertips by Harry Henderson (Chelsea House, 2012)

The Man Who Invented Television: The Genius of Philo T. Farnsworth by Edwin Brit Wyckoff (Enslow, 2014)

Niklas Zennström and Skype by Jason Porterfield (Rosen, 2013)

Seven Wonders of Communication by Donald Cleveland (Twenty-First Century Books, 2010)

Tim Berners-Lee: Inventor of the World Wide Web by Stephanie Sammartino McPherson (Lerner, 2010)

Who Was Alexander Graham Bell? by Bonnie Bader (Grosset & Dunlap, 2013)

Websites

About Telstra – Telecommunications Timeline
http://www.telstra.com.au/abouttelstra/company-overview/history/tele-communications-timeline/
Telstra, an Australian telecommunications company, shares a telecommunications timeline from 1830 to the present featuring historical photos.

BBC Primary History – Famous People: John Logie Baird
http://www.bbc.co.uk/schools/primaryhistory/famouspeople/john_logie_baird/
Meet John Logie Baird—the pioneering engineer who invented the television!

Kids Work! History of Telecommunications
http://knowitall.org/kidswork/etv/history/index.html
Chart the history of telecommunications from the telegraph to digital television using a clickable timeline.

ShoreTel – History of the Telegraph in Communications
https://www.shoretel.co.uk/history-telegraph-communications
Take an in-depth look at the history of the telegraph, complete with links to technological diagrams, interactive projects, and educator lesson plans.

Smithsonian National Postal Museum
http://postalmuseum.si.edu/activities/
Learn more about the history and resources of the postal service as you play games, watch videos, and create your own artwork.

U.S. Federal Communications Commission – Kids Zone
https://transition.fcc.gov/cgb/kidszone/history.html
Read the fascinating history behind the radio, television, cell phone, and other telecommunications inventions.

Index